MONITORING
STATION

MONITORING STATION

SONJA RUTH GRECKOL

UNIVERSITY
of **ALBERTA**
PRESS

Published by

University of Alberta Press
1–16 Rutherford Library South
11204 89 Avenue NW
Edmonton, Alberta, Canada T6G 2J4
amiskwaciwâskahikan | Treaty 6 |
Métis Territory
uap.ualberta.ca | uapress@ualberta.ca

Copyright © 2023 Sonja Greckol

LIBRARY AND ARCHIVES CANADA
CATALOGUING IN PUBLICATION

Title: Monitoring station / Sonja Ruth
    Greckol.
Names: Greckol, Sonja Ruth, author.
Series: Robert Kroetsch series.
Description: Series statement: Robert
    Kroetsch series
Identifiers: Canadiana (print) 20220455082 |
    Canadiana (ebook) 20220455090 |
    ISBN 9781772126792 (softcover) |
    ISBN 9781772126983 (PDF)
Subjects: LCGFT: Poetry.
Classification: LCC PS8613.R424 M66 2023 |
    DDC C811/.6—dc23

First edition, first printing, 2023.
First printed and bound in Canada by Houghton
Boston Printers, Saskatoon, Saskatchewan.
Copyediting by Deanna Janovski.
Proofreading by Mary Lou Roy.

A volume in the Robert Kroetsch Series.

University of Alberta Press is committed to
protecting our natural environment. As part of
our efforts, this book is printed on Enviro Paper:
it contains 100% post-consumer recycled fibres
and is acid- and chlorine-free.

University of Alberta Press gratefully
acknowledges the support received for its
publishing program from the Government of
Canada, the Canada Council for the Arts, and
the Government of Alberta through the Alberta
Media Fund.

For Small and her future

Everyone has had someone breathe for them. Until the first ga(s)p. For air.

Do our cells carry this epigenetic memory of a form of sharing and exchange, a modeling of a "we" that we can take into our varied practices?

—M. NOURBESE PHILIP

Contents

First—Chill—then Stupor—then the letting go

—EMILY DICKINSON

Because of Ourselves

Because of Ourselves

flung front skidding knowing certainly not where not when
black ice ahead

poorly wired into the world but the salt spoon is at hand
and the masking tape and giving birth opened a bracket
my syntax dapples every day with that moment in the mirror
that travels farther than it appears

ıbodies at rest do not move toward each other unless the strength
of their attraction surpasses inertia their velocity
determines the traj…ejectory unless probability shakes the scaffold
symmetry absented left gaping a fish gasping for wordlift
rigour gone
trolling gleaning afraid of showing up not knowing

at 9:09 p.m. Aug 15 2015 Katie was 99 years and 159 days old
(a site makes the calculation)

we held her blue hands warm-blanketed round her cold feet
her breath faltered quieted rage long gone ferocity expired
unwound

I was her issue and I am her issue
and I issued a daughter who has her high forehead

memory lights her way   No!

memory lights our way

no research no boundary just bonds mourning
we weep precisely we cared for each other lament being no more
poised to chisel each other greater and other
than us in another turn obliged to harbour us

we know we knew we remember
felt body lived body—the trunk is where the emptying recurs
dizzying scintillating withering

tree rings mine and hers entwined loops of sensation
infant swaddled against her tight arm toddler straining
for the horizon over her muscular shoulder child helping her dress
when the sensation passed from soft to hard—
the basque corset shaped those '50s women—
while I was just a hard skinny girl

orbits wobbled
jagged space surrounded rounded us away

I was not an easy teenager she was not an easy mother
our spheres discordant we grew distant not in spite of ourselves
but because of ourselves
emptiness has shape and volume—felt body lived body

4

looking on that face
I signed papers attesting that body to which I had been issue
from which I was issue lay there right there in that birch box
both alone
leaving

placing the cold kiss the rose unceremonious—she had been
a farmer a gardener proudly coaxing growth then reaping pruning
harsh close to the root us

watching the box into the vault there is no gaping maw just roar
flames burst eclipsed clanging door engulfs body movie images
displaced
dendrites crackle allegory escapes me
grief is
fear is not

○

at the front of the line we share her life in ours
vitals birth parents husband siblings—seven predeceased—work
travel take relief in due diligence

in my body there is a blank
I found it once held its shape my mother her mother
our unknowing

no sobbing in the family room
story and threnody granddaughter's soprano startles sings
us apart loving : : loved folded into the fold and unfolded again
when the carriage of the end ends and it does
and it does and it is an end with shards carried from that end

empty now
surrounded by my own escape bodied and dis-
after the fact how after it is the matrix rent strained tears
meanders shorn arrive on the ledge white lilies white lilies
now here not there then there not here
lying beyond past our meridian

after great pain

Overhand Knots

möbius strip is a long strip with a twist
joined end to end

a line drawn lengthwise from the seam
meets at the join

but on the other side if continued meets
at the starting point

the strip cut along the centre line yields
one long strip with two

full twists when cut the strip yields
two strips wound

round each other with two twists
cutting a strip with three

half twists divided ties in a trefoil knot
unravelling to eight

half twists—overhand this
knot of molecular loss

allegory returns

a formal feeling comes

The new beginning inherent in birth can make itself felt in the world only because the newcomer possesses the capacity of beginning something anew, that is, of acting.

—HANNAH ARENDT

Our ʻOumuamua

2017 Nov 29 @ 8:30 a.m.

Freya Kate born hungry among those who eat heartily
suckles with gusto catapulting me besotted
confused
tracing a line longer
my mother's name honours her where I could not—not a repair
but relief like a stent not quite effective not quite necessary
serving a line longer

                                                        It's complicated
Nothing like it has ever been seen before

Ethereal interstellar visitor   no
no   just an infant our infant unusually elongated—strong material
avoided breaking apart passed gravitationally unbound
expelled from her encumbering planet
whelms our galaxy solo

                                                        our 'Oumuamua

Have you ever watched the moon rise?
Appearing larger and brighter crowning slow—
most impressive imagined looking out for our newest—
silhouettes admire the dawn

Tonight a nearly full Oak Moon spools our sphere
white clouds spinning earth lights people in Barcelona's streets
blue oceans visible sunset to sunrise ever rising
straddles borders   Fleeing Rohingya deemed stateless
My sphere jiggers where no other more spectacular
separation glided past into my homeworld but red atop the volcano stars
planets the corona's diffraction draws my eye

                                                        right there!

What's happening on the horizon?

Here in moonlight small droplets fused
aligned behind the centre most galaxies have a single nucleus

Umbral shadow near the midpoint strikes subtle shading eclipsed
fiery corona surrounding lighter outer shadow follows an adventurer

                                        newborns stare

Surface probe shadows puddles of infinity
sun-facing side wings open flit
dark interiors hide new scars formed around dense lores
embedded deep visible jest of the familiar—
skyscape is blush

Narrow energetic jets blast from hidden infant star
layer regions shining months long but tonight promises to be another
good night to get caught in a meteor shower
the streaks

Raise your arms if you've seen aurora

Two nights   clouds mostly
ribbon of highway a lone figure majestic sighs—
regret turns to sadness we knew we were not to be close jagged—every
few minutes the sky sparked

                                    tenuous this repair

A low groan radiates my body transiting generations
you can tell which hip mimicked hers—
the meteor streaks—

                                        I wonder if my mother felt wonder
if she did none did she convey

Without comfort   with effort
turned inward she orbited closed even hot to harbour life
her fears scoured my cooler distant planet

I wonder if I felt wonder
if I conveyed wonder

In moments of pivot one sees one's life
differently even as her|my daughter sees my|her life differently
through dust of generations enthralled by this northern nightscape
shower's radiant ancestor meteors register a small planet

Parallel tracks appear to diverge behind the nebula casting penumbral
shadows funnelling sighs in thick hot dust streams anxiety dreams
loneliness

Crusted flinty tough she chewed us

Mourned the daughter she didn't know the grandson she never had
husband she accused who stood with others who stand accused as
mothers are tough weak bright angry soft mean silent
pick any three

                                                  go ahead!

○

Rocky and sun-baked parents in their orbit claim
the perihelion in rapid motion faint or resolute
mercurial infant flashes closest to planet Mother

                              Grandmothers get to be over the top

Spectacle in this micro universe plumed from the first stage
tiny space fish mouth puckered
collects larger creatures backlit

Settling struggling against their grain against their complex want
driving drought thriving against withered
                              hope facing hope

One Year Now

facelight frames illuminates night sequences moon trails concentric
exposures stack along digital horizons round their fixed celestial pole

our axis minuscule shining from foil shook into orbit
below geostationary below the space stations   here!

                         on earth
the birthing room soundproofed

                      for whom?

launched painfully few will appreciate the endurance the solitude
the certain unpredictable outcome that lifted two navigation satellites
whose mission landed and encircled her one year now

composite of fears lifts me well above plummets me well below
threshold of reckoning

                      I am frightened
                         write it!

more so and less over this year news is dire resistance is palpable
stepping onto the new street   we face our culpability

                      wrath of Freya

                      ○

starlight whittles cool cosmic mountains
read peaks whittled for profit   protest staunched
you will ask *how could you let this happen?*

growing cavity filled with the spectacular stellar nursery forming
open lustre of stars fairy ten light years tall spews radiation hotter than
fire

you loved me and you let this happen? what did you do?

I canvassed voted cycled recycled drove an electric car
demonstrated boycotted flying was mine skiing was mine
no kayak canoe

today the moon is near Mercury and Mars is on its way past Neptune and
I am quailing here at 43° 40' 24" N | 79° 21' 5" W | 92 m
above sea level on the shore of Lake Ontario without visible night sky
but for the moon

now we are more more smiles quips smart talk runny noses shining
bigger fears bigger complications

reliving my night terrors—child of Hiroshima and bomb tests
convinced the world would end—mothering with Reagan and Brezhnev
desperate to protect your mother in the event of nuclear war—

                                                  fear of my fears

and recognizing these grand fears attend certainty
                            I walk white each night without fear
                            shop without scrutiny
                            travel subways unnoticed
reveal myself my place: one who claims space

face to face with precarious life still I breathe better
coal-fired plants shuttered the city breathes better

                         my granddaughter is without lead in her blood:

Grassy Narrows people carry six decades of mercury poisoning
generations of Minamata disease documented and resisted
600 Indigenous communities boil drinking water with fuel oil
absent power lines
                                    knew it know it

yearning for the large stumble on the small stuff
                                 small things thing up

oxytocin rushes my cells waterfall of Orion trapezium in the star-forming
region laced with filaments of fear anxiety for water air cascade of care
Ring of Fire nickel copper chromium bests Breathing Lands
in this now
                                           now

generative impulses inundated probes intricate limits of the viable
opaque to visible life obscured by quadrants of streets over streams
gurgling up in basements concrete evidence of controlling failures

put on your red|blue glasses and float next to the asteroid
lay our heads together on a fuzzy blanket reaching stars

shaped like a spinning top with boulders littering its rough surface
our grasp slipping and flailing reaches orange and red

tiny solar world you
                                              construct us planets
expand into each
                                      settle exploring orbits
                first this house with a yellow door yellow snow shovel

samples of dust from another asteroid streak earth's atmosphere
sooner you will streak ahead from arms strong sinewy but crepey

when the meteor shower peaks in predawn skies now bathe you
your second Geminid sheltered for now from Phaethon's folly

release desire to protect to know intimately the spot where I live
the spot I share with you

fraught with concrete cement wires pipes that sustain my|your life erased
lives undo unknowing to feed to feel ourselves with the earth

                                              fanciful thought that

comforter just visible below the eyebrow cosmic clouds glow-worm
reddish below the Pleiades clutter express blueberry starlight

it's complicated—we don't see ourselves the way others see us up close
not inside still rarer to see anything close stepping into the gap is
dangerous

orbs brighten on the monitor we watch we hover still chuckling

walk walk walk runrunrun

jump!

giggle and screech

sundogs and sun pillars—ice crystals from snowmaking machines
empathy routinely overwhelmed by struggle to keep it together
Mercury leaving its shadow more solar ice halos fewer rainbows

memory eases the present or perhaps leases against a future
implicating more quickly than pasts can absorb forward thrusts—

thrust into a future that can't look like the past

Freya may be the origin of Friday but our Freya is Thursday's child
having far to go—a mixed cocktail of data driving this work along an
axis of anticipation twined with anxiety—forest fires floods rapid rain
ice snow *really you are letting this happen?*

In the last transmission from the solar-powered rover as the bubble's
centre inflates where a helmet-shaped Thor prevails comes up sideways
captures earth's mantle

Extractocene burrow suck expel hurl peel desiccate defoliate stream
away from the shower's radiant desalinate smelt extract separate silt skim
scrape evacuate decoct capitalize

telltale greenish coma thunder seems immanent or even imminent

excited by energetic light from newborn stars our very own
monoceros reflects starlight among her menagerie fox elephant giraffe
frog ascends her own tree star cluster churning mixing clues of gasp and
dust-up startles

                                    grandmothering takes its toll

left the laptop charger in the crib room wondering why *intricate* has
fallen out of use as a verb—*extricate* survives—English no longer
having use for a verb meaning *entangle* or *ensnare*

Perhaps profound naïveté allowed us to elide the usage to *complicated*
and *detailed* to no longer
                                    contemplate complicity

Monitoring Station

In the country of daughters of daughters where peak
cold radiates in the sky *look there!*
small figure approaches gingerly

                                testing her return

consumed by profound restlessness rootlessness Recollects
of childhood trails and trials limn her meander
inedible mushrooms psychedelic
barley wheat

                                              chafe

Homesteads ploughed round archive first faces trace
colonial grid names vanish percolating distant
foundations language lost takes storying
absence expands experience recedes

                                far faint and dim

randomness floats up never to empty Lurching staying vertical
narrow strides in deep tire tracks through snow sprawl
far from cleared avenues moose deer elk traverse
52° 28' 11" N | 113° 19' 14" W | 834 m
captured by night-vision tracking cameras
mediating our wild hydrocarbon nights
beyond the pipeline

                                    monitoring station

Witness landscape keloid from the aerie auguring CO_2 agitates dogs
across the valley where crews reappear January fog
seethes from the Rockies bears oxygen
North China Sea mercury from
Mongolia toxifying Lake
Ontario stew

hope creeps

under the door dispersing clouds By angular coincidence they met they
are there I watch their chef in pigtails yesterday the firefighter
blowing kisses closing the toddler room door
leaves and branches reach
their sky

sweep forward

Naked eyes trace verticals and obliques belayed by climbers on the
translucence spread spider-like navigating the glacier below pale
blue-green agate winter's streaks deep to the impact basin
Horâ Juthin Îmne Lake of Little Fishes
laid deep under wan sun

this now

jets shriek and plume askew ancient terrains as Cassiopeia
turns her chair on Perseus following Andromeda Venus
Mars rule tonight's gravity align my filaments
loop and flare on granite cloven by balsam
spruce and fir where hoof boot

maps streams

dust starts and ends as dust mere stack of microbes obscured
heightens fears small fuzzy patch mosaic stipple scraped
from crumbling walls dates persistence
BCE cluster

                                                    marks time

feeding lakes from the Great Divide where twenty years ago
unceremonious we scattered ash and bone on Neptuak
51° 24' 25" N | 116° 13' 25" W | 1700 m
chickadees nattered

                                                    Mike N

museum panorama 53° 43' 30" N | 113° 31' 57" W | 645 m
tapestries hang warped weft woof tilt oblique obscure silence
we: europeans we: settlers they: blank we: civilizers
bringing sewing machines tableware lanterns
machined fabrics 1950s dioramas drain
slight insight

                                                    loss radiates

floods listless visitor groups early risers assembled for the colonial
play grave marker engraved silhouetted rose ceremonious
mercantile reverence Last settler
generation

                                                    unknowing incised

horror children and dogs sequestered indoors from marauding
wolves starving for game small prey flushed Parents brought
up short by blood pressure or a failed valve diabetic
spikes or melting permafrost and glaciers calving
while we contemplate another site

eclipsed heartlight

in the darkest place cacophony breaches the horizon calibrating
moments not acquit of blame bound to place
reckoning harsh light
fowl January

Wolf Moon

Snippets of Boona's old-country song mustard poultice chamomile
persillé dreams earth visions older than ancient populate cells
daughters carrying gestalt
tissues

redeemable

hidden from clear view glimpsed through veils gas dust
earthly fog spiral arms wind newly born weaves
bind familiars
between

craters and years

nerves sit ceremonious

To perceive matter that casts no shadow, you must search not for its presence but for its consequence.

—ROBERT MACFARLANE

Möbius

What is coming down appears so large still constellated data points gasp
the nation while numerators quail—there's quailing and then
full-on panic facing the camera full—denominators undo they
say "aerosolized"—only scientists thought that word two weeks
ago—perhaps hitching rides motility challenges mortality and
there's a volcanic earthquake in the Canary Islands

Full moon threnody to shattered lives or tattered at the very least while
Zoom cannot avert the plague sans locusts boils frogs or hail in
the immediate vicinity

○　○　○

The passing star falls in everything vanishes we count
ready steady confetti! our Small goes close generating gravity
we pull away disrupting the barnacle
longing wrenches the matrix   right here!
and there!   masses shift across roads in India abandoning the city
grandparents carrying toddlers and pots

The star crossing my dark sheds joy continues
to orbit on the inner edge of giggledust surrounding the notouch
chase heated and glowing long rent my Gma fabric

I'm mad. I really want Gma to come to my house.
Gma is very sad and a bit teary that she can't give you hugs and cuddles.

Rigel Witch Head Flame Fox creature her dreams
haunt her swath of sky born two and a half years streamed her
newborn mother harbouring the nebula dubbed Small pivoting her
bigs' hourglass orbit
this mighty force emits our reflected light

Without touch
the matrix
the
bodytobody
wrap
that warps
absence
warps time
wraps
skin to fascia
to fluid
courses
waving
tufts of
absence

Caterpillar nor butterfly chrysalis imaginal cells pandemic soup hold winged vision but fur a fomite! and fearing the worst my dog my biotic harbours unimagined life but a fomite is any surface! any surface! that might land a virus—pestilence borne by pets or any surface viral hosts loom—rake my amygdala amp panic

Lights wasted up dark sky resolve to predawn's blue hour cast across eastern roof peak resolve to sunrise across a city stilled

Night crowding out crocuses coronal skyscape above the serene square
        wanes aloof telescopic no hint of microscopic near the ecliptic
        Mercury rising the line extends to the horizon city stirs
        minimally—two metres please—where is the common? virtual
        arms reach connect the elusive inner planet very close not
        quite visible in this morning sky

Slightly hazy skies no traffic jam in Toronto just an impressive pile of
        black squirrels frolicking under daffodils raccoons taking the
        Danforth at night leaving no carcasses Venus nestles again
        midst the Pleiades eight years after the pandemic was on the
        World Bank's horizon

The raccoon barred tail and face rules Chester subway entrance at 9 pm
        slowly glances up at passing dogs not unnerved by proximity
        done butt grooming it sidles along unalarmed nature easing
        amongst alerts glowing hot red fearful of breath fearful lack
        spiralling dark vapour lanes orbiting the commons masked six
        feet

○　○　○

Seclusion tweaks my pen yet I feel not sorrow but fear and loss
bereft of touch imaginary arms where Small had been
where nestled absence long down my body memory
requires concentration

tracking loss rainbow pie chart Zoom red regards FaceTime
birthdays email stacks orange Twitter flutters sky lists indigo virtual
xoxoxo
fill days spin pole kiltering echoing
longing body my body on my mother's my daughter's body
on mine slacks loopless

Breath in wiry tendrils wafting visible off the young star clusters skinny
six feet elicits growls grinding each Groundhog Day without
exit midst the columns and curves high dust lines bend shrill
alarm limns uncertainty absorbing minds conditioned to
certainty to the short flyby

Drifting sculpted microscopic legless wingless propelled on respiration
curtailing our aspiration stocks roaring the bull rearing apparent
shapes unsated in stealthy algorithms winged leggy pulse our
deaths

○　○　○

My confidence shaken utterly even as Small rides her scooter
emerging midst the park's new foliage desolate of children voices
how fortunate some of us have been

Not ill-starred quite the opposite
our little trio twirls and swirls skateboard muddy puddles *whoa!*
huggable trees unnamed tower among amenities
recrudescent fears grounding
hang climb swoosh rips my body memory to ache

Fragile as community fragile as nations face the microscopic condensations aerosolizations feverish people not notoriously good with numbers guided by bright naked-eyed statisticians

Bending the curve truing the line curving log or linear breaking opinion asserting expertise binding to a method that iterates requires time and stamina and more time and more trials successive approximations measuring reliability choking on prediction beware small samples and the rush to closure

How many times have you washed your hands today?
ahh you had soap water even hot water but not so much
in parks tents on open grates while you are housed and
others hosed watching the Command Table

Tiny solid particles liquid droplets carbon black smoke from fires earn
scant pause sea salt aerosols typhoon formations swirl wane
unthought desert dusts hurricanes loom sweep time lapse
vigilant in high atmosphere but this miasma runs stealthy on
gusts stalking memory keepers stripping eons of stories

Venus climbing among the Pleiades maps solitary deaths ravaging
Lombardy sorrowing kin sequestered raging grieving rent of
elders—soldiers resisters—interring recall artillery wars strikes
mobilizations

If you could see my life on X-ray under this night sky
would seem ordinary in every way laptops large screen
TV or two fully loaded remotes arrayed fungi books race
books poetry largish children's collection that I read a
generation ago dog conditioned to protect dust bunnies
lurking under COVID restriction become the ordinary I
read exotic stars galaxies hot supernova remnants now
captured by an X-ray of the centre plane Milky Way no
ordinary night

Planet COVID
swerves
detailed charts
belay
institutions fracture
nations bifurcate
no stars lighten
deaths' gravity
witness data drains
out meat packers'
eyes security
guards shot
providing masks
righteous deniers
affixed to greed's
magnetic field
striating violence
buoy theft slavery
stoke my anger
masking sorrow

○　○　○

What kind of fish do you want for your face?
or was it *What kind of fish would you like your face to be?*
either way Small's world joyous figment
sequestered from arms rumbling flailing windmill
not even this once no!
traces short concentric arcs empty

Behind those clouds dawning straight lines array crepuscular
thoughts converging on the other side
of this moment's forbidden hugs and cuddles
radiants hopeful appearing somehow supernatural
anti-crepuscular

Want the heights flying through Saturn's rings time lapse buoyed by
the micro engineering struts and alloy defying space bending
time into this nano arrangement of protein and nucleic acid
disease manifesting across the globe defied by soap hot water
sanitation most don't have watching photos from the Cassini
spacecraft (now cindered by Saturn) have the soap and space
here—in each house on this street and those have it in space—
but the others have not on earth and perish in the trajectory

Pelican Cat's Eye Running Chicken Nebulae birthing star nurseries
others dying process order truncated multiplier of courage or
greed's messier objects failed state boundless on the south flank
or perhaps lower-mass stars about to shed outer layers to shine
bright producing a molecular wind Red Square Boomerang
Tarantula

The solitary bookish child immersed legs dangling
from a Russian poplar or languishing nuzzling horse
sidles up beside me in my wing chair fits herself close
in the curve leans in reading Erdrich weaving an
Indigenous narrative of land theft and woman abuse
against the tales of Buffalo Bill and Annie Oakley
not Buffalo Brigades nor Hunt Laws colonial settler
miseducation Dominion's promise wooded lots rich
loam at NW-25-55-14 W4 landscape absent grid lines
inconceivable

That eye on the left the close one captures fear empties unknown skitters
unknowable arches overhead reflect while the right the far eye
stares at the Milky Way shot from the Atacama Desert where
small town lights glint copper around a rocky lagoon surface
pool distilling lithium to power this laptop no one sheltered in
that place what could go wrong? where El Niño rations water

Men on construction sites unmasked huddled pairs taking the evening's
middle sidewalk young overweight men unfit dismiss Six feet
please! ooze insouciant resentful belligerent their fragility large
and dangerous while capital's heat-seeking logarithms ferret
out slimmer investment for larger margin calculus of return
on risk sheltered behind velvet ropes overriding the calculus of
care

Gaze lands rambles the universe showers viral moments piques dailiness
stealth renders concentric boundaries porous renders touch
violable bodies violable debris long tail curve lashes vulnerable
pen renders visible makes opaque for profit in the ligature of
the moment

○　○　○

Membranes of solitude shield my heartmoments
loss emerges from longing bodies
bright loss

Small virtual preschooler catches balls climbs
ladders scrambles over structures erupts
through glass or video self-making
Who will greet us? leaning into our curves
remade again deserted streets strangers at distance

On the other side of the parabola vertigo cytokine storms lungs whiten
        clots loosen monitors flat-line body bags slip silent curve flattens
        but here this side fear creeps astride another day's reprimands
        erodes will pierces bodies vulnerable COVID spins bodies flung
        twirls besieged from without cloud-like shroud bodies lungs
        filled white wired umbilicus laces apparatus circulating blood
        relieving alveoli complex molecules straining reason to think
        life may exist there ever

Flat empty wraps me this middling day flat to gorgeous
piquant smoked fish dogs straining leashes sniffing
butts piqued by yesterday's robin today Where is her
cargo? geese maintain uniform distances in shifting
currents deniers blunder clumsy silent surly indifferent
cold planets emanating their noxious fear unmasked
devoted to small screens not my fear alone not of
persons but of their oblivion rupturing sociality in the
common's glistening crowd

Piloting distanced COVID streets post-menopausal women recognize
hips' faint cant gaze shifts slight shoulder swag palpable to the
reconnaissance eye decades of discipline of the trained female
public body

Looping Zooms long blue ion-tailed twirling wine and tuna crumbling on
thesis drafts diapers divorce death stroke staged in sophisticated
coffee equipment limning the fifth stage of woman resisting
the sixth filigreed to infant and toddlers safely harboured to orbit
essential services ensuring distancing protecting the front of
the line

○   ○   ○

I can't find the chicks in the Running Chicken's constituent stars
dust storms exist in particularity
cut off from my better self from the self not needing
to smoke not rushing to answer email she;I engage Small
write draw silly faces throw cuddles ricochet dizzy

nebulous inside the push-button espresso life
Zoom talk conversation money for causes physical trainers
struggling to be worthy not delivering Meals on Wheels
taking calls on a hotline
feeling Small's bodyweight absent
sheltered at the front of the line

Solid stone lone
stone deserted
terrain invites
exceptions
resenting
breaches
skating close to
the common but
unable to
transgress
invincibility
spent my
dewlap deepens
the stone
lodges at my
breast

○ ○ ○

Little jugs have big ears the settler child heard
sequestered but not sheltered recalling Aunt Anne's death
Métis families labouring parcels to Europe Korean War
children breathed by iron lungs but hidden
from animal mating and birthing

Small learns her sequester protects us from coughs that could make
us sick watches cautiously
openings tilt

Preschoolers arrayed Hollywood Squares jigger and zoom
charged with no edge-on view no touch beyond their parents
foisted into the bright spiky experiment *doing my work!*
engaging virtual life curated for Small
severed from peer touch reaching multitudes
recalling the '60s toddler searching to change pictures
in the window frame fiftyish now still looking for knobs
zooming drone killings in Yemen Somalia
COVID highjacks my daily NASA photos track M106 masers
measure beyond our Milky Way 23.5 million light years distant
beyond unthought a hundred years ago

Even as humans knew an answer would take 50,000 years messages
broadcast toward the globular star cluster M13 in 1974 ever
hopeful kids shout across the lane rigorously distanced
puzzling abandonment emptiness wraps these aging limbs
chuffed still that humans are adding garlic to bovine stomachs
to reduce methane because cows as a country would be the
world's third largest greenhouse gas emitter someone knew to
check calculations

○   ○   ○

Orbiting close Small veers joy crumples
she whirls away to parental hugs
my arms trailing neural debris eddy emptied

Second generation revisits Spot's hiding places wacky joys
Murmel Murmel jolts Small's expectations already
skewed by absence inspired exposure off the top of the frame
capturing joys with thrown hugs and virtual kisses
flash slicing fears of abandonment in pandemic
family ties not as bright but ever

Small things
thing
to small things
heaving jerking
panic dial to red
stripping
tattered
certainty primal
fear surging
cataclysm
inverts lived
worlds
arrives blotting
the
Flower Moon
unmooring me

Legacy of Hiroshima and Nagasaki in childhood
my certainty that life as I knew it would end before
adulthood or perhaps sensing girlhood's ending in
uncertainty or annihilation; later dread at postpartum
impotence genocidal wars spiralled peripheral to my
contra-gravity web protecting my daughter but now
COVID daily erodes the capacity to imagine blank as
more small things loom large and touch surrenders
floats in a universe of grief torrential in Yarmouk in
Rafah in Cox's Bazar Bangladesh's colonial bestowal
holding loss spliced to exile galaxy of my itchy
heartscab peels to laughter the girl ago chasing pigeons
securing my refuge discomfort weights null at this
scale full at this lux struggling for purchase

Thin and faint this month's ellipse densely darkened umbra strands
    absence masked bracketing the centrifuge missing days moon's
    gap nights cede certainty banditry rises behind distractions
    bandits smile unmasked impervious

Rohingya dying stilled statelessness stranded in bamboo and tarpaulin
    ash and smoke globalism stymied there starving infected old
    people die here dehydrated stranded in their soiled beds look
    long! there is a point so bright it dazzles while caretakers sicken
    and die of small choices multiplied

The kitten with tiny pink and blue bows and prehensile paws like a racoon and I are alone in the creepy-feeling house as it climbs vertically to my height on the sheer glass face of the cabinet defying gravity; ordinarily comforting I try to keep it out of the house, but the tricky bit of fluff keeps getting back in while I'm totally tangled in getting it out, it deftly manoeuvres a large canvas sneaker off to the edge of the stairs making way for nonexistent foot traffic, makes a cozy nest and snuggles down for a nap purring loudly, just like that, with me standing over it perplexed about sheltering it—but why with those claws?—nailing signs asking people to claim their cat with pink and blue ribbons or throwing it out to find its way home—where did those paws come from anyway?—what is my responsibility to this cat and this shared viral encounter and why does it keep coming back before I've decided what to do with it in the last go-round? I awaken befuddled by a kitten in the time of COVID.

In the Cox's Bazar district where three people have confirmed COVID
          where 700,000 refugees are held in camps alongside 3.4 million
          people where there will be more as our sun shines brightly where
          deniers scream for their freedom to nuzzle because they have
          immune systems feeding dark rivers between

Revealing Jupiter's surface over time infrared wraps eyes to deeper
          hotter layers where the planetary storms seethe warp to legions
          precarious denaturalized racialized mothers and grandmothers
          spiked with COVID provisioning without shelter food jobs income
          transport health struggling children surge angrier touched with
          all the blaze the sudden sun discloses which side you are on

○　○　○

Magic Forest Monster *Sam-he-is* ! segues between generous scary
toddler brain rhizomes to monarch to thirsty frog
draining energetic particles feeding pretend
from stellar nurseries to Gma's backyard circling
mud in her CAT hauler
circling bodies spiralling yearn

The sun poured down sticky doors sprung toddlers and scooters and
cyclists and dogs displaying their social distancing knowhow
while parents gently chided Space meaning something quite
different now a measure of community against the torrents
of freedom without responsibility spinning inside clouds
unmasking angry crowds breathing rancour and disease

Close-up frames an imagined field improved lawns lifted potatoes
growing and basil tomatoes chard to feed toddlers as they
scramble for strawberries churning a chaotic vista rhythmic
new green

Every sneeze dry tickle jiggers sheaths of miasma trickling down my body congealing funnelling recrudescent gyre not circle not corkscrew spiralling lines from a bat's wing or a cough efflorescing beginning and ending frictionless neither live nor dead needling the host COVID deems me old

Trajectory fulfilled no back glance thirty-nine years ago I laboured this whole week not hard but enough not to sleep and this was the day I spent tranquilized—large molecules don't cross the placental barrier they said—sleeping on a taut hospital bed on Wednesday with Mary updating the exercise class still labouring she said startled looking at the contractions recorded for the entire week daughter yet insists on her own arc and two days later sluiced the dark passage quick merciful always sky appearing above the horizon is really reflection

Pinecones knobby
sharp slick metal
post
pine needles
prickle
running magic
forests
among the violets
no skin on skin
thrown hugs
no hand in hand
blown kisses
dandelion plumes
aerosol dismay
between us
learning life without
garlic waft or spice
breath stokes need.
manifests luminous

Hubris Quivers Inept

I shall say murder
A white woman apparently Canadian calls the police from Central Park because an African American man videos her rounding on him for telling her to leash her dog and an African American man is choked or suffocated by police officers I shall say murdered in Minneapolis and the military witnessed people dying left on floors wailing for help where they had fallen in long-term care homes in Ontario—artful words slip slither superfluous

Branches of capital
Round back of Saturn's rings A-ring politicians round back to tired rationales offering nothing surrounded by grim F-ring ghoulish figures quivering hubris enlarged by ineptitude police racialized bodies scattering disdain forward rounding back claiming caretaking from black and brown female bodies

If there's a knife
No bright stars surround the moon caught in branches of capital's inner planets excess and desires thwarted in lethal conjunctions of superiority and skin at angular distance from whiteness thrashing for purchase righteousness sleight despoils arouses

Getting our helmets on
Sense through sentences *he could talk he could talk* glimpses green just as his sun disappears they're throwing plastic water bottles over a long path longer wavelengths police have put on their helmets separation of colours lends amber hues *it's a tear-gas canister brother don't pick it up it's hot!* refracts nonsense *we never send a mental-health team if there's a knife* harder to see the flash trapped in vestiges of mastery

Sitting in resistance
The arc bends toward youthful drives for new eye treatments with masks in public space energetic protection for Guerlain Sephora circling my reading under leafy green holding peaceful masked demonstrators bleeding from rubber bullets falling clutching their faces clawing at pepper spray amid smoke tear gas armoured vehicles where aging writers sequestered breathe shallow normal will can should not revive

Struggle for Dignity

Demonstrators bleeding

What will remain? an answer suggests itself over the past week reaching its pinnacle this evening spectacle star formation flanks the villain brandishing a historic Bible having had his way cleared by troops and tear gas sauntering away oozing *it's mine! mine!* claiming mastery over the country generating shearing winds met with people sitting in resistance creating temperature differences in adjoining regions

Cleared by troops

Spirits rise over grocery bags lining sidewalks trashed stores burned not by large tentacle-flailing aliens but testicled zombies manspreading marauding enforce supremacy over bodies conflating God and guns arrayed against epic struggle for dignity against fear against harms squalid and lethal

White world authority

Worlds spin at uneven rates when a human falls twenty-three stories when our conference falls silent for twenty-three seconds when flash bombs pepper spray spin jiggered words fall flat kern lines of disbelief along lines of shelter clanging for frontline workers gravity curves quiet bandages wrap playgrounds yellow

Sheerly arrogant belief

Black and brown people fall by cop gunshots chokeholds white world authority takes knee shielded at the auroral curtain break resolve leak umbrage tired retired in righteous respite this and no more emboldened or stand to attention stanching deadly laws forming new vessels girding harms

Teens egged the grifter

Where COVID on the ground ice crystals in the upper atmosphere nightshining clouds at twilight noctilucent illuminate sheerly arrogant belief in God's hand protecting the Tulsa gathering for tomorrow's Kool-Aid made redundant by bad education racism and poverty—others commemorate the ensnared slaughtered and liberated

Against fear against harm

The premature victory lap staging heroic salvation turns to rambling demagoguery after sunset K-pop teens egged the grifter TikTok shortest night fewer bodies less bedlam likely fewer deaths eclipse the longest night for dangerous promises to foolish multitudes

○   ○   ○

Flamingos arch and jive dolphins bounce scatter Small scoots
curvy streamlines tentatively reviews her before-life
under the stars among dust grains aligned
these lockdown months looping filaments tentatively sating
hungry skin magnetic ecstatic

Finding the same tragedies remain visible in morning skies disingenuous corrupt politicians gutter education lining up patriarchs' resentments along the horizon of tell tragedies stack without coincidence

○ ○ ○

Perfectly right-side-up Small inverts her world
walruses in trees foxes in the pond purple monster distraught
in the magic forest
listens to the willow entreating children to be gentle
with her low-hanging branches
hear her vital under long shadows *you need to listen very carefully Gma*

Planetary nebula NGC 7027 core unknown expelled gauzy blue shells
for 600 years now bursts gassy frames dotted red teeming
absorbing earthlings' reeling rationality empathy literacy
expelling more gases and dust with abandon

Chattering squirrels tall plants random pinholes winkle across the
canopied playground banned empty under slant sun children
learning grass twigs ladybugs beetles mariposas flit light on
the patient still

Uprisings flare and warp this spiral's disk there beyond the edge of the wide frame's faint tidal tail lies deep portraiture your children mine segmented bits and bytes scraping your neighbourhood's clicks and whorls selling your heart rate my blood pressure my sister's lung X-ray your viral load my race ethnicity blank contemplate that and sleep tonight

Our moon is new walking Danforth masked without solar eclipse over
central Africa crossing South Asia and China and ending over
the Pacific Ocean always rising of the night reaches Ecbatana
Kermanshah Baghdad Palmyra Lebanon Spain place names
run out colonial powers shuffle off having seared rings of fire
drought devotion leaving refugees Zaatari Bazaar Yarmouk
Achol-Pii Bidi Bidi Imvepi none COVID protected

The dark shadow SARS-CoV-2 emerged onto planet earth in December
2019 maybe earlier Italian scat (more poetic less accurate than
feces) points to predictive value novel listening device freedom
demands deciding freedom to withhold consent for testing red
light cameras ruin romance

Southern hemisphere Magellanic Clouds dwarf galaxies wreath the
Milky Way's incident perfect airglow swallows wheel low
through dead trees rising toward the east arm's reach belying
the calm lake's inner life blue-green algae slime drips microbes
costumes underarms ambivalent toward hair

That viral load flick digit Google hoovers webs shiny
phone to friends passers-by dinner guests through
the urban deems you worthy of work gives purchase
bright trail captured short beamed by satellite pro-
cessed world contaminating the river draining the salt
pools cutting through the forest powering decillions of
bits your|my gigs leaving you|me limned right here re-
constituted webbed alters speaking raging consuming
scheming loosed from bodies building voices cabled
to profit

Outbound data develops a short anti-tail cleaving the
public trailing our metrics reaping their profits leav-
ing my privacy emptied capturing my desires purple
shoes atomic weight of nitrogen striped bed sheets
recipe for Manhattans returning fulfillment stippled
by ash and grime calibrating pleasures modulating
celebration touchless Siri injests ajouré of yearn

Cat's Eye comes around again haunting symmetries stunning with
false-colour pictures revealing enormous taut faint lines data
wrapping material shrugged from earlier active episodes
haloing faults to outer arrays

The photo of the 3,000 km gash across Mars opened when the planet
cooled billions of years ago manifests human's scant length
and span still without capacity to synchronize for want of
metre stick and mask immediate nearby whereas slime mould
ants and locusts manage with loners to spare

○ ○ ○

Languishing in poetry stars and planets constellating me
looking skyward not wishing to dirty my hands
in the innards of frogs and pigeons the very idea repulses me
still I am stuck feet planted on degraded earth Small's future
learned neglect perhaps only now taking my place at eye-level
with turtles and puffins in her dreams

We venture closer puzzlement crosses her eyes
she knows of germs faint scatter on her giraffe her soccer ball
but two metres have shrunk stilling hugs without sanction
viral loads R number and denominators that seem to elude
innumerates while the streets fill many many-harmed rising

Shirt buttons fumble shoes find unfamiliar feet
hair split long no comfort gleaned numbers accumulate lines
web constellations to myth and mycelium and back
lacklustre thrust of dailiness muffles even scoots and catch

Losing my
lines
pushing
my pile in
hapless
zigs and
zags
without
mooring
words
from the
cosmos
day gone
amiss

○　○　○

Dung beetles disorient in hats or under clouds or polluted
atmosphere losing the Milky Way falling prey
anchoring us in the sandbox under the sprinkler and then...
clarity in a small piece of the critical zone staking tomatoes
learning fluid dynamics from water-filled doggie bags
biodegradable of course

In the prospect of Small's hugs just out of reach
hover aches outfolding futures straddle transgressions
fungal planetary stellar blur I cannot disarm
stranding my joyous giggly pod frizzy with
hugs and cuddles oxytocin unleashes drains dormant algaeic
puddles stagnated in rocky shoals resentments stoppered
flow of flows Small drains touch hunger

Notes

"Because of Ourselves" (as "Mother Loss") and "2017 Nov 29 @ 8:30 a.m."
were previously published in *La Presa*, issues 1 and 6, respectively.

EPIGRAPHS

M. NourbeSe Philip, "The Ga(s)p," in *Poetics and Precarity*, eds. Myung
    Mi Kim and Cristanne Miller (Albany: State University of New
    York Press, 2018), 38.

Emily Dickinson, "After great pain, a formal feeling comes— (372)," in
    The Poems of Emily Dickinson, ed. R.W. Franklin (Cambridge: Harvard
    University Press, 1999), 170.

Hannah Arendt, *The Human Condition*, 2nd ed. (Chicago: University of
    Chicago Press, 1998), 9.

Lee Maracle, *Memory Serves: Oratories*, ed. Smaro Kamboureli
    (Edmonton: NeWest Press, 2015), 193.

Robert Macfarlane, *Underland: A Deep Time Journey* (London: Hamish
    Hamilton, 2019), 56.

Gratitudes

Margaret Christakos edited this work, sprinkling her starburst skill and vision to enlarge my reach.

Brian Dedora and Bill Elleker for carefully winding through these pages with me.

Lee Gould, Donna Fierle, and Bev Daurio for insight and encouragement.

The Wednesday Poets: Jaclyn Piudik, Lynn McClory, and Mark Goldstein for their engagement at critical moments.

The virtual international, national, and local poetry and activist communities that nourish and challenge me.

Ross White, who helms the Grind, in which this work began in August 2015 and which has sustained me through these passages, including the overwhelming initial months of the pandemic.

The many astronomers and photographers that contribute to the Astronomy Picture of the Day (APOD), which focuses my sight across the universe.

The University of Alberta Press staff and reviewers for their generous comments and support.